LANZAROTE

BONECHI

CONTENTS

© Copyright by Casa Editrice Bonechi - Firenze - Italia
E-mail:bonechi@bonechi.it

Publication created and designed by Casa Editrice Bonechi
Editorial management: Serena de Leonardis
Graphic design: Serena de Leonardis and Sonia Gottardo
Make-up: Sonia Gottardo
Texts by Pierluigi Scialdone and Patrizia Fabbri
Editing: Federica Balloni and Patrizia Fabbri
Cover: Sonia Gottardo
Translation: Susan Jane Fraser, Studio Comunicare, Firenze, and Eve Leckey

Printed in Italy by Centro Stampa Editoriale Bonechi - Sesto Fiorentino

The photographs belong to the archive of Casa Editrice Bonechi and were taken by
Andrea Fantauzzo, Paolo Giambone and Andrea Innocenti.

The publisher apologies for any omissions and is willing to make amends
with the formal recognition of the author of any photograph subsequently identified.

ISBN 88-476-1575-5
www.bonechi.com

INTRODUCTION

Centuries ago, for sailors who crossed the mythical Pillars of Hercules and ventured forth into the unknown, challenging the winds and ocean currents, Lanzarote, with its parched earth, was always the first island to appear on the horizon. Located to the north of Fuerteventura and just one hundred miles off the African coast, Lanzarote is, in fact, the most eastern and northern island of the archipelago. As it is only 836 square kilometres, it can easily be crossed lengthwise and widthwise on short car journeys. Only twenty kilometres separate the west coast from the east coast, whereas Punta Fariones, in the far north, is about sixty kilometres from Punta de Papagayo in the far south. Of volcanic origin, it is known as the island of the three hundred craters and belongs to the same continental shelf that supports the little islands that appear to the north of its coasts and Fuerteventura. Despite its large number of craters, Lanzarote is the least mountainous Canary Island. Its maximum height above sea level is 670 metres (Peñas de Chache) and is reached on Famara in the north western part of the island. Its interior is barren, reminiscent of the surface of the moon, studded with small craters, fumaroles and amorphous eruptive formations. The lack of vegetation is due to intense eruptions that have occurred over thousands of years, the extremely dry climate and erosion caused by strong winds that blow off the sea. Very few plants and trees could survive in such a hostile habitat. Apart from the little xerophytes, which are particularly resistant to high temperatures and water shortages, the most common plant on the island is the palm tree which is typical of the Canary Islands and grows mainly in the Haría area. Unlike the other Canary Islands, especially Tenerife, it rains very little on Lanzarote. If this is an added tourist attraction, guaranteeing good weather throughout the year, it is detrimental to agriculture and the island's water supply.

The lack of rainfall is largely a result of Lanzarote's low average altitude and lack of high mountain peaks as the hot, wet currents of the trade winds, encountering no obstacles en route, fly over it at a height, thus hardly affecting its climate.

Man has also had to struggle in order to adapt to the tough living conditions of this volcanic island.

There are traces of primitive man, even though we are not certain about the origin of the indigenous tribe who lived here. In the old native language, Lanzarote was referred to as Titreroy-gatra, or "the red hill", whereas Roman traders who crossed the Pillars of Hercules and came this far called it Purparaia, referring to the the purple hue of a lichen, from which a dye was extracted, growing on certain parts of the island. Its present name has nothing to do, however, with the island's brownish colour, but comes from its first known explorer, the Genoese nobleman Lanzarotto Marocello, who landed there between 1320 and 1339.

Since then many other journeys were made for the purposes of trade and geographical exploration. In fact, countless European traders set sail for Lanzarote in search of slaves and the precious lichen from which orcin was extracted. The first to conquer the island, however, was a Norman knight, Jean de Béthencourt (1360-1425, exact dates unknown). Having received from the Spanish Court an investiture for the undertaking and the faculty to administer and govern the island, the adventurous French knight organized a naval squadron with a crew of about 250 men and, in 1402, he set sail for the archipelago. The first of

the Canary Islands that they came across were Alegranza and, imediately afterwards, Lanzarote. Upon disembarkation on the south coast, between Punta de Papagayo and Pechiguera promontory, he was pacifically received by the local inhabitants. But the illusion of an easy conquest without any blood being spilt soon disappeared.

In the absence of Jean de Béthencourt, who had left for the Iberian Peninusula to recruit troops and ships to extend his dominion and area of exploration, the indigenous tribes rebelled at the tyrannical acts of the conquerors and put up armed resistance. The return of the charismatic French knight and his negotiations put an end to hostilities.

The natives succumbed to Béthencourt's authority and became subjects of the Spanish court, converting themselves to Catholicism following the example of their king Guadarfía, baptized by the French chapelain Le Verrier.

Once it had been conquered, for many years Lanzarote was used for military operations in the archipelago. For safety reasons, a village in the interior which bore the name of Guadarfía's daughter, Teguise, was made the capital.

Even then the coasts were raided by pirates and that is why the

seat of the government and administrative institutions were located far away from the sea.

However, from the 17th century, with increased trade and the diminishing of the pirate threat, the population gradually tended to move towards the coastal areas.

In 1618, they decided to make Arrecife, a large fishing village and trading port on the eastern coast, the capital.

Despite its progressive economic growth and population increase, Lanzarote was never really prosperous until the recent tourist boom.

Until a matter of some years ago, the main sources of income were fishing, goat-rearing and farming, which were barely profitable due to the climate and chemical composition of the soils. In order to limit damage caused by drought, efficacious techniques have been formulated over the centuries: by spreading a fine layer of ash and sand over the area for cultivation every ten years, the loss of dampness from the soils and their impoverishment is considerably reduced. Farming, based mainly on vines, vegetables and certain cereals, is further hampered by strong winds that blow off the Atlantic for most of the year. In order to protect plants, small dry walls are built or holes are dug in the ground. For instance, vines are grown mainly with this furrowing system, which also helps to keep the area around the roots damper. Lanzarote's natural beauties and climatic attractions are further enhanced by its modern way of life, with new tourist and bathing installations, sports facilities, first rate hotels and night-clubs with countless international attractions.

ARRECIFE

Arrecife, the capital of Lanzarote, is a magical mix of sun, sea and enjoyment. Seen here are some views showing how the city of Arrecife has developed a modern and practical style of urban layout in recent years.

This dynamic administrative centre to the east of the island is named after the particular conformation of its coast and continental shelf. Apart from stretches of steep cliffs and rocks ("arrecifes"), there are little islands with indented coastlines that rise up sharply from the sea here and there, forming a crown around the inlets. This seascape must have deeply impressed the first colonizers if they decided to call the village, which they founded at the beginning of the 15th century, after its predominant natural characteristic. For over two centuries, **Arrecife** was only a humble fishing village with very limited trade. Its coast was constantly threatened by pirate raids and its interior never produced enough to justify significant exports. At the time, Arrecife was the port and access to the sea of the primitive capital, **Teguise**, just as Santa Cruz de Tenerife was for La Laguna. The situation started to change at the beginning of the 17th century. It was in 1618 that Teguise was razed to the ground by a horde of Berber pirates. Even though it was a seaside town, Arrecife underwent less damage. It was then decided to make this small coastal village the capital, and, in no time at all, it became the most densely populated centre on the island. Arrecife's development was also facilitated by the fact that the Spanish imperial fleet was finally beginning to defeat the pirates. Therefore the coasts of the Canary Island were made safer and trade could commence under easier conditions. At the same time, the production of farm products, such as grapes and wine, grew.

Nowadays Arrecife boasts a population of almost 30 thousand inhabitants and represents over half of the local population. Its main source of income is fish-

Above, the lofty silhouette of the modern Arrecife Grand Hotel, situated 6 km. from the airport.

ing both in terms of fresh and processed fish. Thanks to Arrecife, Lanzarote possesses the third most important fishing fleet of the Archipelago, after Tenerife and Grand Canary. As a result, an important fish freezing, preservation, deep-freezing and salting industry has developed for export to Europe and elsewhere.

The demographic and economic growth of Arrecife has not changed the appearance of the town, which is old and modern at the same time, with skyscrapers towering above the little white colonial houses which have been proudly preserved intact.

One day is sufficient to visit the town, also because its real charm lies in the intimate atmosphere that pervades the streets of the historic centre, the avenues and the squares of the most modern area, along the sea-front or in the public parks.

The sea has always been the main economic resource of Arrecife and has given rise to a range of activities related to fishing.

SAN GABRIEL CASTLE

Built for defence purposes right in the middle of the sea, for centuries it was a fortified outpost in the struggle against pirates. From its walls, one can see the entire bay, including the coast-line of Arrecife and two small islands known as *Islote de los Ingleses* and *Islote del Francés*. Built according to a square plan, it features grey stone bastions equipped with cannons which were often fired to drive off pirates. It was built in 1574, when Philip II and his huge Empire were at the peak of their glory and wealth. In 1586 it was razed to the ground by the bold Algerian pirate Morato Arraez, despite strong opposition from soldiers and civilians, including numerous women. Historical chronicles and annals relate that, when they were no longer able to defend the castle and pirates started penetrating into the fortress, the women present at the time preferred to take their lives than fall into the hands of Berbers possibly becoming as odalisks or slaves in distant lands. It took four years to collect sufficient funds to rebuild the castle. It was redesigned by the Italian architect, Leonardo Torriani, who included a draw-bridge between the town and the island, where the **fortress** now stands. It is known as *Puente de las Bolas* due to the granite balls placed on the strong pillars that flank it. It reflects the severe Herrerian style in vogue in Spain during the second half of the 16th century and was named by its creator, the architect Juan de Herrera.

The "Puente de las Balas" which links the city to the small island where the mighty San Gabriel Castle stands (above).

Details of the 16th-century San Gabriel Castle.

11

CHARCO
DE SAN GINÉS

This large lagoon opens out between the coast and the town of Arrecife, where the blue of its waters blends in with the sky. Due to its waterways, the town is known as the "Venice of the Atlantic". For centuries, fishermen have exploited this charming natural port, which enables boats and small launches to be moored, and drawn out of the water to carry out repairs and maintenance.

CHURCH OF SAN GINÉS

The town's most interesting church is dedicated to the patron saint, San Ginés. Built during the period of the conquest as a small retreat where Catholic monks and missionaries could go to pray in solitude, it owes a great deal of its present appearance to the restoration and enlargement carried out during the 18th century. With its elegant square *tower*, crowned by a charming *dome*, and grey stone and plaster walls, it is a typical example of Canary Island architecture during the colonial era.

SAN JOSÉ CASTLE

Larger than San Gabriel, it rises on the northern outskirts of the town and overlooks the Bay of Marmi and the port of Naos. It was commissioned by the enlightened King Charles III of Spain and built in 1779. It was intended to strengthen the defences of Arrecife and enable safer trading conditions. Unlike many other Lanzarote and Canary Island fortresses, it was built during a period in which the threat of pirate attacks had diminished considerably, even though naval battles had intensified in the Atlantic Ocean between imperial and colonial powers for the dominion of overseas routes and markets. However, history relates that Charles III had it built to assuage the sufferings of the population at the time. 1779 marked a bad harvest which, accentuated by difficulties in importing foodstuffs, led to famine. In order to provide employment for poverty-stricken peasants King Charles III commissioned it to be built; it was then called "hunger fortress" in memory of the episode. Work continued between 1774 and 1779 involving much of the local population. The mighty San José Castle was built according to a

The pretty San Ginés Church (above) and a view of San José, the other castle that protects Arrecife.

Further views of the 18th-century San José Castle, a well-endowed fortress built to protect the city, and today an impressive home for the International Museum of Contemporary Art.

plan, the curved side facing out over the sea, dominating *Puerto de Naos*, one of the spots where ships could more easily find shelter thanks to the renowned tranquility of the sea here. In fact, however, the **fortress** never had the chance to combat enemies at all and on the whole was simply used as an arsenal, a military function that it continued to fulfill until 1890. It was then abandoned for

a considerable length of time until in 1974 the eclectic and famous local artist, César Manrique, tireless painter, sculptor, architect, ecologist and protector of monuments, chose the fortress to house the planned **Museo Internacional de Arte Contemporáneo** (MIAC) where important works of modern artistic movements were to be collected and exhibited. Manrique personally super-

vised both the task of restoring the castle and the organization of the museum to which he donated many of his own paintings as well as some from his own private collection. MIAC was opened on 8 December 1976 and is today a prestigious international institution exhibiting masterpieces by the greatest contemporary artists, such as Bacon, Botero, Dámaso, Domínguez, Francis, Leparc, Manrique, Millares, Miró, Picasso, Rompó, Tápies and Luis Féito.

CÉSAR MANRIQUE

Versatile and highly creative, this artist is one of the greatest surprises that awaits us inside the International **Museum of Contemporary Art** installed in **San Juan Castle**. Born in 1920 on the island of Lanzarote, for years Manrique focused his attention, with growing success, on plastic and figurative arts. Right from his childhood days, he felt the need to mould colours, shapes and space and to materialize the fantastic creatures that emerged from his imagination and his dreams. When César was a young man, the Canary Islands were cut off from the international artistic world and could only offer him their enchanting seascapes and volcanic land parched by the sun. His destiny lay elsewhere in various, distant lands. In Madrid, César won a scholarship at the Academy of Fine Arts of San Fernando, where he graduated in painting and drawing. After about three years in the United States, he returned to Lanzarote in 1968. His creative activities encompass all sectors of figurative and plastic arts: painting and sculpture with works of a highly innovative abstract style and an interest in town-planning and architecture, which induced him to shape space according to man's needs, pursuing criteria of harmony and balance with nature. It was not by chance that he was called an "ecological artist". As from 1972, he formulated an ambitious model urbanization project, applicable to Lanzarote and the other Canary Islands, that includes the safeguarding of landscapes, the harmonious distribution of buildings and green areas and, lastly, the construction of single-storey homes in a homogeneous style. Even his sculptures affect the landscape and urban areas; they are both decorative and interpretative at the same time. One of César Manrique's works not exhibited in a museum, but located in a magnificent natural setting near Mozaga in the centre of the island where it is visible to all, is the famous Monument to Fertility, also known as the Campesino Monument (1968), a touching homage by the artist to the rural culture of Lanzarote and to the islanders who have always had to fight and struggle to survive against a hostile nature. It is a huge sculpture made from differently-shaped white stones that form a fantastic figure 15 metres high, surrounded by some old agricultural tools, intended to represent a peasant with his cattle. Nearby, and also a product of Manrique's creativity, is the interesting Farm

Museum, *a perfect example of Lanzarote's traditional local architecture, its white-washed buildings with green painted doors and windows surrounding a pretty courtyard. Thus Manrique, already well-known and appreciated for his paintings, also became famous internationally for his interventions in natural settings. In Berlin he was awarded the World Award for Ecology and Tourism, and in 1978 King Juan Carlos I awarded him the Grand Cross of Civil Merit, followed two years later by the Gold Medal for Fine Arts (1980). With a succession of journeys, paintings, books and new projects, the prizes and honours increased and included the "Europa Nostra" Prize, also for his environmental work on Lanzarote, the* Teide d'Oro *and the prestigious* "Fritz Shumacher" *award from the Stifftunf FVS Foundation of Hamburg. In 1988 he began the restoration of the house in Haria and moved there in 1990 intending to transform the house of Taro di Tahiche into the Foundation that he was already planning to create. The same year his last work on Lanzarote was opened – the* Jardin de Cactus *– formerly a gloomy disused cave of volcanic sand that the versatile artist had transformed into a wonderful hothouse of magnificent cacti. In 1992, on 25 September, César Manrique died in a tragic road accident only a few metres from his Foundation. Today he is buried in the cemetery of Haria and even his grave is delightfully unusual: instead of a headstone, it is marked by stones and volcanic earth and instead of flowers, only succulents and palms.*

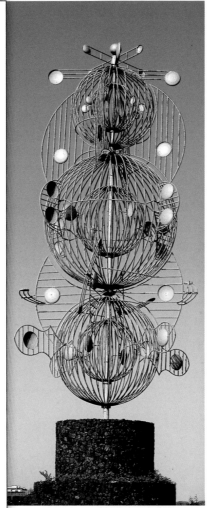

CÉSAR MANRIQUE

The aim of the independent César Manrique Foundation, perhaps the most appreciated and popular institution on Lanzarote, is to promote, preserve and exploit the ideas and works of this famous artist. The centre is housed in the legendary 'Taro de Tahiche' located on the road that leads to San Bartolomé. The story is told that on returning from the United States to live on the island in 1968, Manrique was quite astonished during his first journey in a car, to see a fig tree that had taken root and tenaciously clung to a solidified bubble of black lava, last

remaining evidence of the final lava flow of the historic series of eruptions that shook the island between 1730 and 1736. Manrique was determined that precisely there, where the tree had so determinedly thrust its roots, he would build his new house. The house was entirely in the local style and tradition, but with one unusual feature: the rooms on the lower of the two levels, situated below ground, were excavated from five enormous and adjoining volcanic blisters. This singular residence, where the artist went to live in 1988, was therefore a genuine work of art

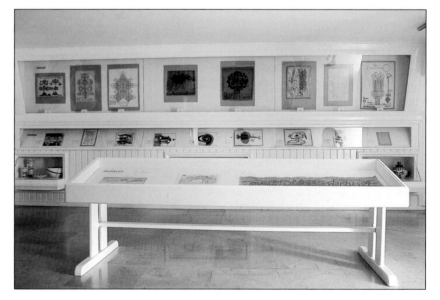

in itself as well as being the perfect testimony to César Manrique and his way of interpreting the relationship between architecture, art and nature as a flawless and harmonious fusion of all these elements.

However, as a residence it was also rather demanding as its unique fascination attracted many artists, politicians and simply individuals who wanted to admire it. Manrique therefore soon decided, sadly yet without

regret, to move to a simpler but more peaceful house, dedicating the 'Taro de Tahiche' to a more suitable role as the home of his new Foundation, opened in March 1992. Today this important institution preserves

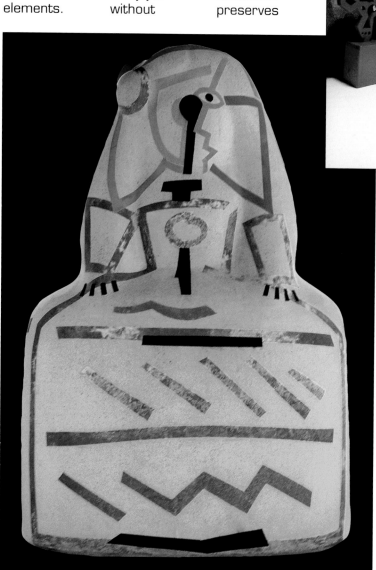

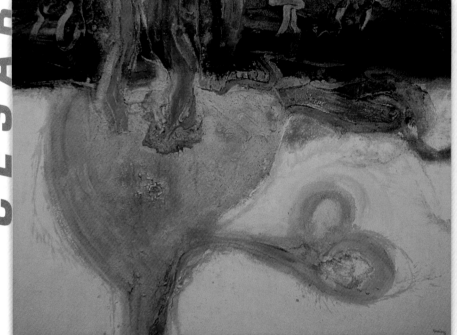

MANRIQUE

CÉSAR

and exhibits not only
the sketches, plans and
designs of Manrique but
also a collection of works
by contemporary artists
which belonged to him. The

Foundation therefore now
represents an important
cultural reference point
for the whole island and is
quite prolific in its initiatives,
organising conferences

and seminars, as well
as publishing important
works on art, history and
environmental conservation.

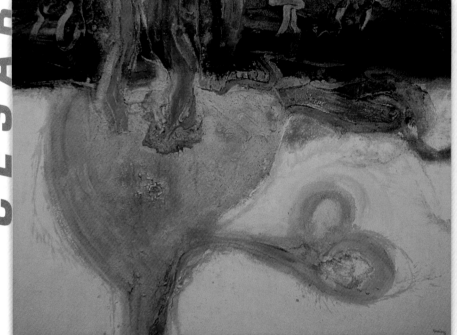

Here and on previous pages internal and external views of the Foundation,
inspired by Lanzarote architecture, some of the rooms and some
of the works exhibited.

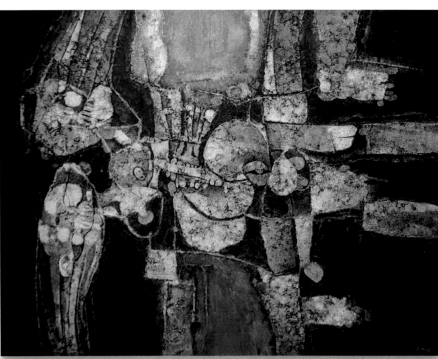

PLAYA HONDA

Lanzarote is endowed with many splendid beaches, but without doubt the fine Playa Honda, an immense strip of golden sand almost 2 km long, is worth a special mention.

It is a unique experience to walk along this shore in a relaxing atmosphere created by the rhythmic sound of the breaking waves and the invigorating heat of the sun allowing one's thoughts to wander freely and lose themselves in the far horizon. The Playa Honda beach, easily accessible and perfect for those who enjoy swimming, is also flanked by a panoramic seafront called the *Aventino Marítima*.

Among the most attractive of the island's large beaches, Playa Honda is sandy, sunny and has a splendid seafront walk.

TANIT ETHNOGRAPHICAL MUSEUM

At *San Bartolomé*, at precisely the geographical centre of the island of Lanzarote, is a rather unusual museum entirely dedicated to the great heritage represented by the customs, traditions, culture and daily life of the native population of the island, a heritage that has developed most significantly over the last two centuries. José Ferrer Perdomo and his wife, the artist Remedios Quintant Reyes, were able to turn the hope of creating such a museum into reality by dedicating an entire 18th-century house to it. The house was owned by the Perdomo family and is a typical example of Canaries domestic architecture, located in a charming urban setting surrounded by palm trees, tropical plants, benches, fountains and white towers.

For many years the couple enthusiastically collected all kinds of objects, stories, information, memoirs, traditions and evidence of a way of life from the time of the Guanci to today, with the intention of creating a veritable treasure trove that would be saved and protected from inevitable dispersion as time passes. These items form the core collection of the Ethnographic Museum which was finally opened by the Perdomo on 18 February 2000. It was named *Tanit* after an ancient Carthaginian deity, the goddess of love, good fortune and fertility, whose symbol, which also became the symbol of the museum, was found sculpted on a stone block from *Pozo de la Cruz* at *San Marcial del Rubicón* on Lanzarote.

THE TEGUISE COAST

North of the administrative centre, beaches and bathing establishments alternate for kilometres between the blue of the sky and the volcanic interior, forming a crown of gold oases. It is without a doubt one of the stretches of coast used to best advantage from the touristic point of view. Exploiting marvellous climatic and natural characteristics, modern villages have been built offering first-rate hotel service and equipped with all sorts of accessories, including sports facilities. By and large, the balance of nature has been maintained and the flora has been increased with lawns, flower-beds, a wide variety of plants and lofty trees. This stretch of the coast is referred to as the Teguise Coast, because it lies mainly within the *Teguise* municipality. It commences a few kilometres from Arrecife, starting from the *Los Molinos Apartments*, a series of bungalows and little houses surrounded by greenery, amusement parks, bars and restaurants, and sports facilities. *Hotel Las Salinas*, an elegant five star hotel, is to be found near this residential, tourist village. Subsequent holiday resorts feature all the same characteristics and provide the same comforts and impeccable service. They are busy all year round, even in winter, when the climate is still very mild. Tourists in search of sun and warm beaches enjoy their stay in a continuous whirl of emotions and night life.

Two views of the Teguise Coast, the third largest tourist area of the island, immediately to the east of the port of Arrecife, with the typical, brilliant white buildings.

TEGUISE

What used to be the island's capital is situated in the interior, in a barren plain burnt by volcanic eruptions and only sprinkled with touches of greenery. On leaving Tahiche, one heads northwards and encounters en route a charming village called *Nazareth*, with whitewashed houses and patios that are a mass of flowers.

Teguise, which is named after one of Guadarfía's daughters – the last native to reign before the conquest – is one of the oldest, most traditional towns on the Canary Islands. During the 15th century, it grew from a village into the heart of the political, administrative and religious life on the island. In many ways, it is similar to *La Laguna*, administrative centre of *Tenerife*: they were both established far from the coast as a safeguard against pirate raids and incursions by colonial powers, enemies of Spain; later on, both lost their title of capital to large coastal towns, and they both have that distinguished, superior air typical of colonial towns founded by the Castilians overseas. The austerity of **churches** and **convents** is softened by the elegance of old noble palaces and the grace of stone or brick houses with large windows, plastered walls and charming balconies typical of the Canary Islands.

The landscape around Teguise and left, the Square of San Miguel showing the lovely church of Our Lady of Guadalupe.

Even though it is several kilometres from the north and east coasts, Teguise did not entirely escape pirate raids. For istance, in 1586, the Algerian pirate Morato Arráez attacked the Arrecife coast, razing **San Gabriel Castle** to the ground and heading inland as far as Teguise. The place where dozens of townspeople were massacred, including women and children, is commemorated by a street name, *Callejuela de la Sangre* (Blood Alley). True to form, many buildings were burnt and demolished. Also the **Church of Nuestra Señora de Guadalupe**, dating back to the fifteenth century and originally built in Gothic style, was severely damaged. Restoration and renovations have changed its appearance completely. On the whole, however, Teguise's monumental heritage has been well preserved over the centuries. Apart from **Nuestra Señora de Guadalupe**, the town features many other prestigious religious buildings including the old **Convento de San Francisco**, which houses a precious engraved *statue of the Saint of Assisi*, perhaps attributable to an unknown Genoese sculptor.

But Teguise is also famous for its music and folklore. For centuries its name has been linked to various musical instruments, including the timple, a five-string guitar invented locally. The Canary island instrument has a narrower, longer sound box than Spanish and Portuguese guitars which most probably influenced its design. Teguise's tradition of musical instruments reached fame thanks to the skill of the master craftsman Simon Morales Tavio, who jealously handed down the secrets of his art to his sons.

The Sunday market in Teguise

Teguise is one of the main tourist and cultural attractions of the island and the most traditional, popular and best-known event held there is without doubt the chaotic and colourful *Mercadillo*, a large open-air market that dominates the life of the town every Sunday morning and public holiday. A mass of stalls overflowing with the most diverse merchandise offers a wide range of goods from local merchandise to interesting crafts products and local delicacies that are well worth tasting. The festive atmosphere is often

further enlivened by the performances of folkloristic groups of singers and dancers dressed in delightful local costume.

28

SANTA BÁRBARA CASTLE

Before leaving Teguise, it is worth taking a look at its surroundings and climbing up to the peak of the nearby *Guanapay* vulcano. From the top of this old crater which has not erupted for centuries, you can see the entire Teguise valley and lateral mountains. It is a barren landscape, studded with stones and brown-grey volcanic rocks, and only interspersed here and there with stretches of green fields. The view sweeps the horizon as far as the coast and even further, beyond the blue of the sea, to glimpse the dark outlines of Fuerteventura and the smaller islands. On the summit we can admire the old **fortress of Santa Bárbara**, also known as **Guanapay Castle**. It was built during the 15th century for defence and sighting purposes. Due to its favourable position which does not permit easy access, it was possible to sight pirate ships miles off, no matter where they appeared on the horizon, and give the alarm well in advance. This gave ample time to arm themselves and take refuge inside the castle walls, organizing defence and resistance to a siege. This fortress was like a stone sentinel that watched day and night over Teguise and its surrounding villages. Built according to an irregular square plan, it was restored and partially rebuilt at the beginning of the 16th century by the architect Leonardo Torriani, by order of the Emperor Philip II.

The imposing structure of Santa Barbara Castle perched on the heights of the Guanapay volcano.

PLAYA DE LAS CUCHARAS

There are many beaches dotted along the southern coast of the island, but one in particular provides an absolute paradise for lovers of a sport that – more than any other – has made Lanzarote famous: windsurfing. On the Playa de las Cucharas on the Teguise coast the colourful sails skim amidst the waves, appearing and disappearing as they catch the wind. Indeed, when the wind is particularly strong only skilled and expert athletes should venture out. On Playa de las Cucharas, however, the wind drops for a few hours and this is the best time for beginners, providing an excellent opportunity to learn the sport. The beach is also extremely well equipped for fans of windsurfing, with centres where boards, rigging and sails can be rented as well as offering storage for one's own equipment and, perhaps most important of all, rubber dinghies provide continual surveillance and assistance.

One of the most famous beaches on the Teguise Coast is without doubt the popular Playa de las Cucharas, surrounded by small traditional houses as well as the unusual structures of large tourist residences.

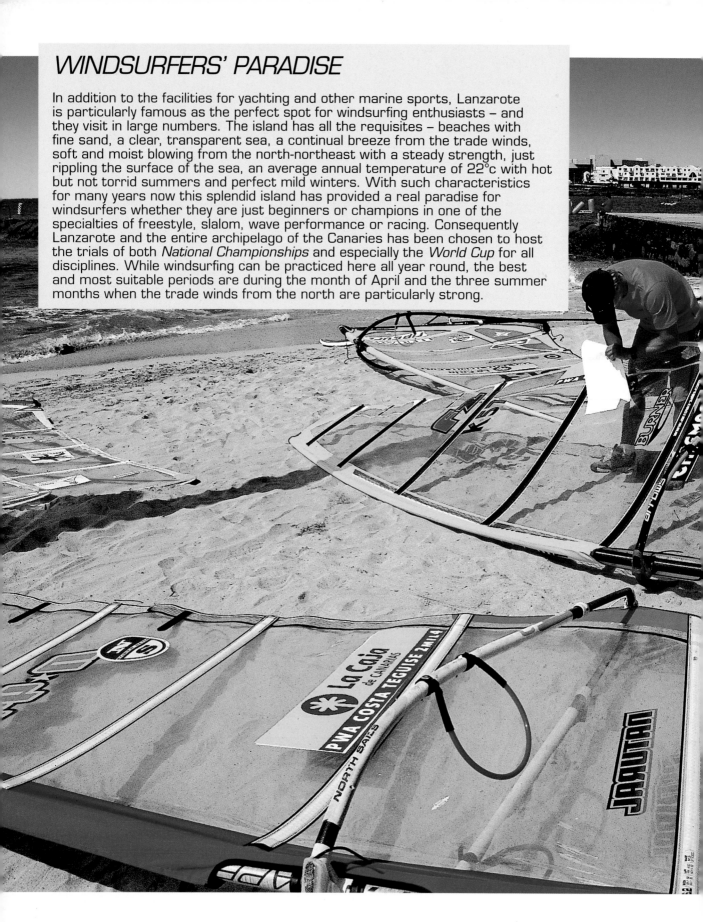

WINDSURFERS' PARADISE

In addition to the facilities for yachting and other marine sports, Lanzarote is particularly famous as the perfect spot for windsurfing enthusiasts – and they visit in large numbers. The island has all the requisites – beaches with fine sand, a clear, transparent sea, a continual breeze from the trade winds, soft and moist blowing from the north-northeast with a steady strength, just rippling the surface of the sea, an average annual temperature of 22°c with hot but not torrid summers and perfect mild winters. With such characteristics for many years now this splendid island has provided a real paradise for windsurfers whether they are just beginners or champions in one of the specialties of freestyle, slalom, wave performance or racing. Consequently Lanzarote and the entire archipelago of the Canaries has been chosen to host the trials of both *National Championships* and especially the *World Cup* for all disciplines. While windsurfing can be practiced here all year round, the best and most suitable periods are during the month of April and the three summer months when the trade winds from the north are particularly strong.

GUATIZA

THE CACTUS GARDEN

Providing another spectacular attraction on Lanzarote, the dramatic garden of cactus plants at Guatiza is a natural masterpiece resulting from the remarkable inventiveness and profound environmental concern of César Manrique. Situated in the lunar landscape of an enormous amphitheatre of black volcanic rock and dominated by an ancient mill, some 9,700 cacti of all shapes and sizes stand in magnificent arrogance. Admirably arranged amidst sparkling waterfalls and neat pathways, a total of 1,420 species from all over the world flourish happily, the brilliant colours of the cacti providing a pleasant contrast to the dull grey of the volcanic sands.

Heading eastwards in the direction of Teguise and then northwards, one comes across Guatiza, which was clearly named by its indigenous inhabitants. It is a farming village like many others, without any great monuments and art treasures. Its main attraction lies in its surroundings and the crops that have been planted. Before entering the town of Guatiza, but especially on the road to the village of *Mala*, the road crosses a wide expanse of greenery, which makes one feel quite overwhelmed: hordes of cacti, grown close together, with large oval blades forming abstract geometrical designs. But why so many cacti? Are they indigenous or were they planted? To find the answer, approach a plant and look closely at its blade-shaped leaves. You will notice that they are full of little insects, belonging to one of the many species of cochineal insects, which come from Mexico and are useful for the manufacture of carmine. This precious natural dye can be obtained by drying and making powder from the insects, which are killed with systems that do not change their chromatic characteristics and chemical composition, including steam. Several thousands of insects, weighing about two kilograms, are required to produce about a centigram of carmine. The consumption of this bright purple substance, which was once widely used in cosmetics, dyeing and the food industry, has decreased considerably due to fierce competition from low-cost synthetic products.

TAHICHE

On leaving the capital and heading towards the interior towards *Teguise*, after five or six kilometres, we come across a village with a clearly indigenous name: Tahiche. It is located in a barren plain at the foot of the 300-metre high hill of Tahiche. It is an old farming village even though today it has become the area in which many inhabitants of Arrecife have built little villas and country houses for relaxation in contact with nature. Due to its magmatic origins, the ground is brownish, but the landscape is still very luminous thanks to the whiteness of houses and the green of surrounding gardens.

A journey to the interior of the island of Lanzarote: left, the strange desert-like environment in the area around Guatiza, with immense areas of cactus which naturally constitute the main feature of the dramatic garden created by César Manrique around the famous Guatiza mill. This page, views of Tahiche (above) and Cuevas da los Guanches (below).

THE GUANCHES CAVES

Part of the central area, from approximately Tahice to Harfa, is of great historic and archaeological interest. Due to the natural formation of the ground, many ancient dwelling and burial-places of the natives of the island are concentrated here. As in other Canary Islands, the indigenous inhabitants of Lanzarote preferred to live in caves rather than in huts made of wood, stone or other materials. A typical abode of Lanzarote is the "casa fonda" (the sunken house), consisting of an underground cave of volcanic origins. It is a long, narrow passage with two openings and a vault that is often only one and a half metres high. Therefore its inhabitants were forced to bend down or go on all fours and to live under poor lighting conditions. The most fascinating, mysterious vestiges of the ancient indigenous civilizations, however, are the "queseras", wide tunnels dug into the rock whose exact function is not yet known. It is generally believed that they were sacred places, where religious rites and ceremonials were performed. Some mistakenly believed that they were large reservoirs to collect rain water; the "queseras" are open at both ends and certainly could not have been used as reservoirs to store the precious liquid in such short supply on the island.

LOS JAMEOS DEL AGUA

This is the name given to the large caves of volcanic origin, which have been shaped by nature over the centuries and, to a certain extent, by the hand of man. They are to be found in the north of Lanzarote, where the island tends to taper. As they are very near to the coast, they lead into the sea through deep, unexplored underground tunnels. One is overwhelmed by the beauty of the place: colours, darting reflections and stone architecture and sculptures combine to form a magic play on designs and figures. One of its inhabitants is an ancient shellfish, a large, white, completely blind crab. This species has been preserved only in the dark recesses of these caves and over thousands of years the white crab has lost the colour of its shell and its capacity to see due to the poor lighting inside the caves.

Los Jameos del Agua: an entrancing corner of paradise, and a wonder of hidden and unspoilt beauty.

Its natural beauty has been enhanced by a series of first-rate facilities: apart from restaurants, bars and dance halls, a series of small swimming pools allure tourists with their crystal clear waters.

The spectacular beauty of the natural scenery around Jameos del Agua has been superbly highlighted by creating comfortable and elegant structures that are not only suited to the needs of tourism but also harmonise perfectly with the surrounding environment. César Manrique, the creator of the project, was responsible for the design of the man-made structures, and he also planned the gardens, walks, terraces, pools, restaurants and even a theatre with a capacity of one thousand spectators, inside the complex of volcanic caves.

CUEVA DE LOS VERDES

This cave forms part of the intricate network of underground tunnels and natural caves, seven kilometres long, which joins the *Corona* volcano to the sea. As mentioned previously, this labyrinth of underground passages and caves, which includes Jameos del Agua, is originally volcanic.

It was formed by the solidification of lava and gas flows from the eruptive openings that created tunnels extending as far as the sea. *Green Cave* owes its name to the colour of moss that has clung to its walls and vaults for thousands of years.

In the past, it was the ideal refuge for inhabitants of the neighbourhood who could escape being captured by

Cueva de los Verdes, a miracle engineered by nature itself with a pathway some two kilometres long in the heart of the volcanic formation.

39

pirates by hiding in the deepest recesses until the danger had passed. The labyrinth of tunnels, underground passages and lava formations provided excellent defence, transforming every corner into an impregnable fortress.

Green Cave is a real wonder of nature not only due to the whimsical, bizarre shapes of the rocks or the play of light and colour, but also owing to the optical effects produced. At some points, we get the impression of chasms that open up in front of us. At others, the spectacle of the vault and walls appears to be turned upside down in a magical mirage of expanding space. All these effects are due to the immobility and purity of the waters that flood the cave and function as a mirror, reflecting the image of the overhanging parts in a mirage of space and volume.

Cueva de los Verdes, a miracle engineered by nature itself with a pathway some two kilometres long in the heart of the volcanic formation.

ORZOLA

Situated at the furthest north-eastern point of Lanzarote are some old fishing villages which have now developed into attractive residential centres. Among these is Orzola, a delightful village that offers the chance to enjoy peaceful sunny little beaches as well as savouring delicious fresh fish and exquisite seafood. Orzola is the northernmost village on the island and every day a ferry departs from here linking Lanzarote to *La Graciosa* and the small islands of *Roque del Oeste* and *Roque del Este*. With the other islands of *Montaña Clara* – small and volcanic – and *Alegranza* – also volcanic and the most northerly – this group forms the *Chinijo Archipelago*, strictly protected since 1986 by the status of *National Park*. Today only La Graciosa is inhabited and elsewhere nature reigns supreme with unspoilt beaches, rare vegetation, numerous species of seabirds and a myriad of fish that delight diving enthusiasts.

Orzola, a historic fishing village clinging to the rocky coast at the north-eastern end of Lanzarote, as well as being a delightful spot famous for the fresh fish that is available in the restaurants, is the traditional departure point for the ferry across to the nearby island, La Graciosa.

Low white houses, colourful fleets of fishing boats, a long stretch of cliffs and towering heights of volcanic rock that seem to plunge into the depths of the blue sea of the Canaries: this is the delightful scenery along the coastline between Punta Prieta and Punta Fariones, the northernmost point of Lanzarote. Mirador del Rio is a spectacular viewpoint on the spur of a high rock face. This wonderful natural beauty provided further inspiration for César Manrique's endless creativity.

MIRADOR DEL RÍO

The far northern point of the island, known as *Punta Fariones*, protrudes into the ocean like a pointed spear. Together with the south-east coast of Graciosa, one of Lanzarote's satellite islands, it forms a sound about two kilometres wide, known as *El Rio* (The River). It is worth climbing up five or six hundred metres to be able to enjoy the view from a rocky spur, overlooking the strait known as *Mirador* (Belvedere) *del Río*, which juts upwards and out to sea like the prow of an enormous space-ship. At the most favourable point of **Belvedere**, one can sit at the tables of a bar-restaurant and admire the magnificent natural setting through windows embedded in the rockface. The largest island, which is visible almost in its entirety, is *La Graciosa*, a barren, desert-like fishing location studded with volcanic rocks and small extinct craters. Further on, one can see the dark outlines of the islands of *Montaña Clara* and *Alegranza*. The cliffs of Belvedere rise steeply out of the sea along a short stretch of the coast, forming a bare, vertical rock-face without any sign of vegetation. With its massive structure and view, this is certainly one of the most evocative tourist spots of the Canary Island archipelago.

The extraordinary natural fascination of Mirador del Rio, a spectacular panoramic viewpoint on the tip of a high rockface, provided further inspiration for César Manrique's continual creativity.

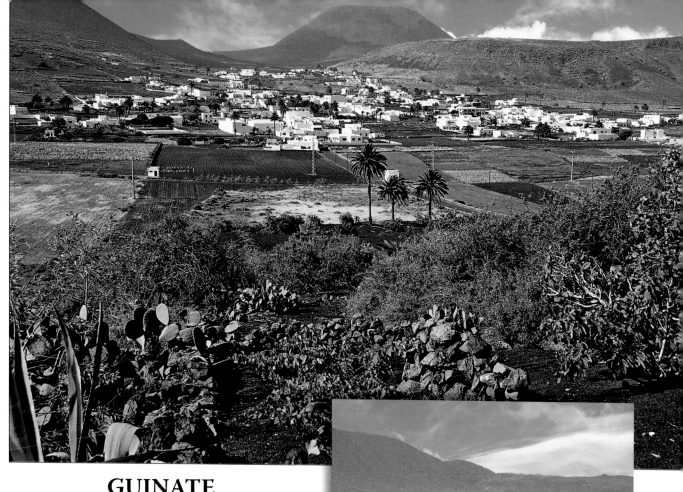

GUINATE

In the north of the island, at the foot of *Mount Corona*, an impressive volcanic cone and one of the highest peaks on Lanzarote, is Guinate, a traditional agricultural centre and peaceful village that enjoys a stupendous view across to the nearby island of *La Graciosa*. There is a fascinating **Tropical Park** here too.

Guinate, an attractive village nestling between sea, sky and volcanic rocks.

The Guinate Tropical Park covers an area of more than 45,000 square metres set against the background of the rocky cliffs of *Famara*. The Park is home to over 1,300 exotic birds and animals living in large airy cages immersed in the natural environment and enhanced with ponds, waterfalls and gardens. A range of tropical plants flourishes all around as well as examples of the native flora of Lanzarote and a magnificent cactus garden.

In this fascinating park with its lush groves, little lagoons, palm trees, waterfalls and numerous cactus plants, live hundreds of birds that are native to the Canary Isles.

Flora

Despite its wide variety of plants and trees, the vegetation on Lanzarote is not as lush as that of the other Canary Islands. As Lanzarote's physical and climatic conditions are quite homogeneous, only certain types of vegetation are suited to growing there. The dryness, lack of mountain peaks and chemical composition of its soils lead to a prevalence of xerophiles – very hardy and resistant to high temperatures, – a wide variety of bushes, algae, lichens and hardy annuals, which complete their entire biological cycle within the space of one year. The areas formed by masses of solidified lava, known in Spanish as malpaíses, produce the Lanzarote "bejeque", the "botonera", with beautiful silvery leaves and yellow flowers and a delicate daisy of the same colour. Furthermore, it features plants that only grow in inhospitable spaces such as the rare "guayadil", which hides in the recesses of the northern rocks. One of the most commonly found trees on the island is the Canary palm, mainly concentrated in the Haría area.

Flora

The dark, fertile volcanic earth of Lanzarote encourages a healthy vegetation that produces a spectacular number of multi-coloured flowers: pink, in the case of Cistus symphytifolius (below, centre), and Lavatera acerfolia (previous page, right), or wild mallow, and Campylanthus salsoloides, better known as romero marino, all species native to the Canaries; yellow and red in the case of Alpina zerumbet (previous page, centre); red for the well-known Euphorbia pulcherrina (above, right) which decorates our houses so splendidly and better known by the fascinating and rather illogical name (for a tropical plant) of the 'Christmas Star'.

The flora of Lanzarote is extremely varied and ranges from cactus (previous page, left, a detail of Euphorbia canariensis) to plants of more arid climes (below, right, is a Euphorbia obtusifolia), to some rare bushes such as Sonchus canariensis and Euphorbia balsamifera, and some slightly frondy trees (such as Echius aculeatum).

One of the most impressive plants belonging to the island's flora is without doubt the majestic Canaries' Dragon (or Dracenaena draco, (above, left) a tree-like plant that has inspired numerous legends and which it is said can live more than one thousand years. The name comes from the blood-red sap called, not surprisingly, "dragon's blood" and renowned for its therapeutic properties.

HARÍA

On leaving the breathtaking landscape of *Mirador del Río* and descending southwards in the direction of Haría, the road winds inland, parallel to the long mountain range that separates it from the sea. In this area there are no mountain passes nor access to the coast; in order to go south, therefore, we have to keep to the western slopes of the mountain range which are most picturesque: water erosion has given rise to deep furrows.

Haría is very thinly populated with just three thousand inhabitants per almost 150 square kilometres. The village stretches into a valley which boasts the largest palm-grove on Lanzarote. However, it is just a shadow of its former self, before it was devastated and burnt by pirates. The town itself is not of particular interest from the historic and monumental point of view, but it does offer attractive landscape and architecture, with white-washed houses as a protection against the sun's rays.

Quite unspoilt by the overwhelming forces of tourism, the traditional white houses of Haria shine in the heart of the Valley of One Thousand Palms.

ERMITA DE LAS NIEVES

Standing in isolation among the rocky slopes of the island's highest peaks that dominate the north-east coast is a small white 18th-century **chapel** built on the spot where, centuries ago, the Virgin is said to have appeared to a young shepherd. Known as the Ermita de las Nieves it is now a place of prayer and meditation immersed in total silence. Not far away is one of the most spectacular panoramic viewpoints of the entire island providing a splendid view over the beach of *Famara*, far into the distance towards *La Caleta* and even beyond.

Not far from Peñasbdel Chache, the highest peak on Lanzarote, at a height of about 670 metres and surrounded by a landscape of rocks and volcanic terraces, the little chapel known as Las Nieves Hermitage stands out.

PLAYA DE FAMARA

Impressively situated at the foot of the imposing *Risco de Famara*, a gigantic rock formation that reaches a height of 600 metres and forms a mighty, steep cliff, the Playa de Famara is one of the loveliest beaches of Lanzarote. Broad, and stretching as far as the eye can see, for over 9 kilometres, and always quite breezy (it is almost impossible to use umbrellas and loungers), the long waves break on the beach and have an undertow of several metres. Looking not unlike a fjord, yet almost a tropical beach, at the southern end is the tiny village of *La Caleta*, a picturesque group of white houses and sandy roads. The sea is fairly cool and usually wavy, but it is possible to walk long distances without interruption on the soft sandy seabed. Although the particular features of this beach do not lend themselves to windsurfing – the type of wave is not suitable and the wind is too gusty, except perhaps for occasional fearless experts – for precisely the same reasons the beach is a real surfers' paradise and a cheerful, continual fleet of surf boards can be seen riding the waves.

The long curve of the sandy, pebbled Playa de Famara stretches far into the distance. Constantly beaten by winds and with strong sea currents, this natural paradise is not recommended for either lovers of windsurf or bathers who like to strike out from the shore.

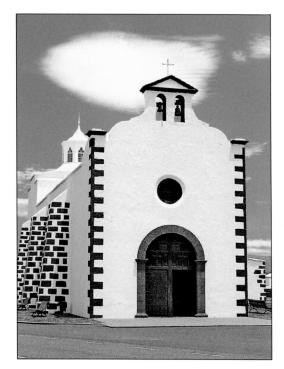

ERMITA DE LOS DOLORES

According to tradition, in 1736 when Lanzarote was devastated by volcanic eruptions, a Franciscan Father lead a procession bearing the *Virgin de los Dolores* to the continual flow of hot lava, promising to build a chapel if the merciless destruction of the land would only end. And the miracle happened. Legend relates that some 40 years later the Virgin herself demanded that the promise, until then forgotten, would be fulfilled when she appeared to a shepherdess and asked her to insist the chapel be built. Work began immediately and continued for nearly a decade on the little **church** of the Ermita de los Dolores just outside the village of *Mancha Blanca*. In 1824 the Virgin – now venerated with the new and significant name of the *Virgin of the Volcano* – was proclaimed patron of the island when once more her image, carried in procession, miraculously succeeded in halting a terrible eruption. Traditionally honoured with gifts and prayers, magnificent celebrations take place honouring the Virgin around Her feast day of 15 September.

The people of Lanzarote are particularly fond of the pretty little church renamed the Ermita de los Dolores, between Tiagua and Tinajo.

TIAGUA

A small inland village, Tiagua is almost in the centre of the island, on the road from *Arrecife* to *Tinajo*. The northern part heading towards the *Soo* area, is volcanic earth which has been transformed into farmland producing potatoes, grapes, melons and large quantities of watermelons. It is a vast area known as *El Jable*. A couple of hours suffice to see Tiagua and its surrounding area. The highlight of one's visit will no doubt be the **sanctuary of Our Lady of Perpetual Aid**, dating back to the 17th century. Its interior features outstanding works of art, including a priceless silver *lamp* hanging in the central aisle.

Despite the tough and rugged land around Tiagua, a small village in the interior, the inhabitants have found sufficient resources to considerably develop the agricultural crops while still using the most traditional of methods.

"EL PATIO" AGRICULTURAL MUSEUM

The "El Patio" Museum is housed in one of the largest and most typically traditional farms on Lanzarote. A working farm until the late 1950s, it was subsequently restored according to a plan developed by César Manrique and takes the visitor on an intriguing journey through more than 150 years of history and peasant culture. Inspiration for the initiative perhaps arose from a historic event that took place in 1845 when farmers from the village of Tiagua asked if they could also cultivate a vast area of land belonging to the Marquis de la Quinta Roja, Francisco de Ponte y Llorena, that was particularly fertile and, until then, not exploited to its full potential. This was the start of an important and stimulating experience that offered a vital contribution to the development of agriculture and resulted in the opening of El Patio

Agricultural Museum on 5 January 1994. In this authentic, original setting, the museum provides an opportunity to appreciate the architecture, traditions, objects, products and customs of Lanzarote long ago.

Windmills, perfectly restored peasant houses, donkeys, goats, a famous dromedary, cellars, and walls of volcanic stone – this amazing and highly original open-air museum takes the visitor on a journey through time to discover the traditions, customs and way of life of the island inhabitants before tourism began, at least partly, to change things.

TINAJO

This is one of the most unusual villages on Lanzarote, with white-washed houses and slightly rounded chimneys reminiscent of an onion bulb. It lies inland, just off the coast and next to the *Parque Nacional de Timanfaya*. Despite its unfertile land, its inhabitants have done their best by covering it with sand, conserving the dampness at the roots of the plants and limiting the progressive drying out of the soil. Despite its lack of monuments, Tinajo boasts a fine **church**, dedicated to *San Roque*, containing two valuable works of art: a wooden *sculpture* of the *Virgin of Candelaria* by the Tenerife artist Fernando Estévez, and a figure of *Christ* attributed to the sculptor Lujan Pérez.

Above, the church dedicated to San Roque, in Tinajo, an unusual village with some quite original architecture. Below, a lovely view towards La Isleta.

LA ISLETA

Near Tinajo, between *Punta de los Cuchillos* and *Soo* desert, it is worth visiting the seaside resort of *La Santa* before concluding our tour of Lanzarote. It is an old fishing village whose very name evokes its ethereal nature and spirituality.

Its major attraction is a large tourist complex, called *La Santa Sport*, which boasts good facilities and lagoons whose natural beauty has been enhanced by wellkept flower-beds, flower-boxes and tree-lined avenues. Facing this stretch of the coast, a small round island is wedged in the bay, forming a narrow arm of the sea.

It is known as *La Isleta* and, apart from its evocative countryside and tropical charm, it offers excellent deep-sea and shore fishing. The surrounding sea-beds are relatively shallow and abound in fish. Lastly, there are no dangerous sea currents, making it an ideal spot for divers.

Long beaches and a sea perfectly suited to windsurfing thanks to a constant breeze, la Isleta and the coast of Lanzarote opposite are pleasant tourist resorts with excellent services such as those of the futuristic centre, La Santa (above).

LA GERIA

A small inland farming village, La Geria is famous for its vineyards. It is situated in the heart of a volcanic area, in a stretch of brown ash and solidified lava, with only flecks of green from the vineyards. Dominated by extinct craters, over the centuries it has been destroyed several times by flows of red hot magma.

However, man has persevered in his struggle against nature to salvage fields for crops and land on which to build. Its inhabitants are hardy, patient people with a rugged, proud appearance.

With skilful crop-growing techniques, they have planted huge vineyards, despite environmental hazards. In this dry area which is almost always subjected to strong Atlantic winds, they have dug count-

less large circular holes, protected by low stone walls. Inside these walls, they have arranged vines, which produce grapes in abundance and wine for export purposes. Even if there are no irrigation canals and rivers in the area, the soil conserves its dampness thanks to a fine layer of sand and ash in the inner part of the holes. Its landscape is quite unique because it gives the impression of a large battlefield, covered with trenches and devastated by bombs.

Some views of the rural area, La Geria, covered with vines and other forms of cultivation.

YAIZA

On leaving La Geria and heading south-west, we come across Yaiza. The pre-Spanish name, as in the case of many other towns on Lanzarote, is of indigenous origins. Far from the sea, this white farming village has always lived in silent isolation: founded by Spanish colonials, it has remained almost unchanged in time, hardly touched by progress and changing fashions. The tourist boom has not radically changed it, as in the case of many villages on the island. Holiday-makers, in search of sun-kissed beaches and beautiful seascapes, only stop over briefly in Yaiza. Its most interesting monument is the old **sanctuary of Our Lady of Remedies**, rebuilt during the 18th century with white-washed façades and sloping brick roofs. A point of interest: in the *cloister* of the church, is the only example of American bamboos on the island of Lanzarote.

The pretty and neat little village of Yaiza, with its bright white church dating from the 18th century (above) is surrounded by a bare and stark volcanic landscape.

PARQUE NACION

North of *Yaiza* lies the largest volcanic region of the entire Canary Island archipelago. Known as the Parque Nacional de Timanfaya, it covers approximately 200 square kilometres and occupies the central-western part of the island. It looks like an enormous platform gradually sloping towards the ocean, with an average height above sea level of just over 200 metres. Here one can find a wide variety of volcanic material dating back to remote geological ages. However, the more recent surface layers go back to the great eruptions of the 18th and 19th centuries, well-documented by eye witnesses and the government council. One of the most interesting accounts was handed down to us by don Andrés Lorenzo Curbelo, parish priest of Yaiza: on the 1st September 1730, between nine and ten o'clock in the evening, he heard a hollow, lacerating roar which shook the very foundations of the village, while the earth opened up, pouring forth columns of fire hundreds

of metres high, dense, acrid sulphur smoke, ash and terrifying tongues of lava. At the beginning of 1732, the eruptions reached such intensity as to drive away all the local villagers, who took refuge on Grand Canary Island, guided by their parish priest, don Andrés Lorenzo Curbelo. The countryside of this part of Lanzarote was literally devastated: green valleys, pastures and hilly slopes where cereals and vines were once grown were transformed into an enormous sea of lava with petrified waves, a desert of grey and blackish dust. Numerous isolated farmhouses and some villages had been literally swallowed up by the magma, without giving their inhabitants a chance to escape. After a period of calm lasting almost a century, in 1824 a number of craters – including *Tao* and *Tinguatón* – became active once again.

On crossing this sort of no-man's land, we get the impression of being transported in a time machine to the dawn of history, before matter had been entirely shaped by the divine will. The morphology of the landscape was not only influenced by the direction of the lava flows but also by Atlantic winds.

Blown by the strong winds coming off the ocean, the volcanic material hurled into the air settled in the strangest, most bizarre fashion. To venture forth

into this arid, desolate area is a unique, unrepeatable experience. One can even visit it on the back of a dromedary, supplied at the entrance to the Park. Caravans are formed, in this way, and, accompanied by a specialized guide, they follow a route across spots with magic names such as *Valle de la Tranquilidad*, *Barranco del Fuego*, *Manto de la Virgen*, *Montaña de Timanfaya*, *Casa de los Camelleros* and, a slight distance from our itinerary, *Montaña Encantada*. During our visit, we can appreciate the intensity of the region's volcanic activity. A matter of a few centimetres below our feet, the temperature is about 400 degrees centigrade.

Small pieces of wood stuck into cracks in the ground catch fire almost instantaneously to show how close we are to the layer of magma in a liquid state. Here and there fumaroles and blowholes send up thick clouds of white vapour.

There are numerous other points of interest: apart from the Islote de Hilario, where one can make use of cooking facilities exploiting the natural

As well as actually seeing and experiencing the phenomenon at first hand, (such as the extremely high-temperature steam jets that gush fiercely from fissures in the ground) the modern information centre, opened in 1996, is well worth a visit. In particular, the multi-media exhibition that reveals and explains all the various aspects of this natural wonder, is especially interesting.

heat of the earth, there is a place called the *Cup of Chocolate* due to the brown colour of the lava when it overflows from the edges of the crater and solidifies. Everywhere, thousands of shades mix and blend in together: ochres and yellows, reds, browns, greys, chestnut and countless others. Vegetation is sparse and consists of plants that can survive in such a hostile environment: mainly mosses, algae and a wide variety of lichens.

There is also very little in the way of fauna: rats, wild rabbits and the Haría lizard, apart from about twenty different types of birds.

EL GOLFO

Further north of Los Hervideros, beyond a small red mountain called *Bermeja* (Vermilion), a splendid natural bay, El Golfo, opens out. The area is barren and thinly populated. Farming and crop-growing cannot be carried out because of the ruggedness of the ground and its lack of minerals. Here one beholds another of Lanzarote's wonders of nature: inside the bay lies a small lagoon with clear, emerald-green waters. Separated from the sea by ash-coloured sand dunes, it looks like a precious jewel that has dropped from the sky and landed in a crater which has been eroded over centuries by the sea. It is an oasis of peace and surprising colour effects which have remained unspoilt by tourism. It is worth refreshing oneself here and taking in all the beauty of its wild nature before heading for other parts of the island.

Some delightful views of the wild natural landscape around El Golfo, where there are beaches, black volcanic rocks, a small green lagoon and a crystal-clear blue sea.

JANUBIO SALT-WORKS

On the west side of the island, in a large lagoon well suited to its purpose, a series of tanks for salt production has been installed.

At a distance, it is eye-catching: an enormous reverberating chessboard inserted in a brown landscape only dotted here and there with the green of bushes and shrubbery. These are the largest salt-works on the island. The evaporation and subsequent deposit of salt crystals follow a relatively quick process, which requires a great deal of sea water, whose salt content is about three percent. Apart from its charming wind-mills, the area features the ruins of an old lookout tower and a magnificent beach with brownish sand.

Striking views of the extensive salt works created at Las Salinas del Janubio.

LOS HERVIDEROS

On leaving Janubio salt works and following the coastal road northwards, the seascape becomes increasingly rough and uneven, with large bizarre rock formations protruding into the ocean. We come across an area called Los Hervideros, where it is most certainly worth stopping to admire one of the most unusual aspects of the island. Its name, in fact, comes from the gurgling and bubbling of sea water in the rocky recesses of the coast. The waves break upon the rocks with such a force that spray and foam fly up into the sky. This is the real meeting point between the four elements of nature because the fire which pours forth from the entrails of the volcanic mountain, Timanfaya, under a clear blue sky, has spread into the sea, giving rise to fantastic lava formations. Here the creation of the world and matter seems to have come to a halt. It gives an overall impression of incompleteness, potential, yet only partial realization.

Los Hervideros, showing the grandeur of the natural scenery created over thousands of years by heavy lava-flows which solidified on reaching the blue waters of the ocean.

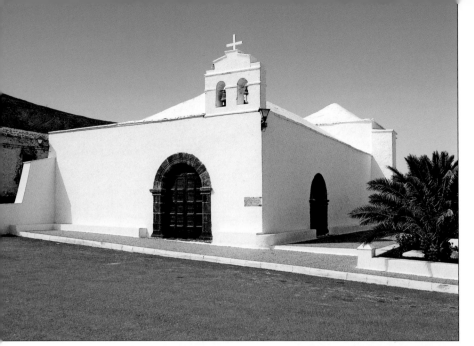

FEMÉS

In the vicinity of Yaiza, but on the opposite side to the *Parque Nacional de Timanfa*ya, lies a charming village, by the name of Femés The sea is not far off, as long as one does not go northwards, yet its influence is mitigated by the hills and volcanic cordillera that surround the village. The most interesting monument of Femés is without a doubt its elegant **church**. It features smooth, white walls in keeping with the best Canary Island architectural traditions. It was built on the site of the old **Cathedral of San Marcial de Rubicón**, which was destroyed during the 16th century by English pirates.

Femés, not far from Yaiza, is a simple and elegant village, as is reflected in the traditional, unadorned style of its church.

PLAYA BLANCA

If we head southwards from Femés as far as the southern tip of the island, we cross an area called *Rubicón*, which is a series of hills and dales. The most stunning part overlooks the sea forming a half moon. Here the steep, rocky coast of slopes leaves ample space for the soft, light coloured sand. The first beach that we come across from the west, immediately after *Pechiguera Promontory*, is Playa Blanca. It is one of Lanzarotes' best bathing areas, because apart from its favourable climate, tourists can stay in modern, comfortable hotel complexes. The most important centre of Playa Blanca is a village that has only recently been transformed from a typical Canary island fishing village. In this paradise of clear waters and tropical-style white beaches, we have everything that we could possibly desire for a relaxing, fun-filled holiday. First rate hotels, restaurants, swimming-pools, sports facilities, bungalows immersed in the vegetation, discotheques and clubs invite tourists to relax completely and enjoy the exciting night life that Playa Blanca has to offer. Ferry-boats leave daily from Playa Blanca's little port for the nearby island of *Fuerteventura*. If one has time on hand, it is a golden opportunity to explore the archipelago further.

Playa Blanca, one of the favourite resorts of the island.

LAS COLORADAS CASTLE

This small fortress stands on the south coast near *Punta del Papagayo*, between *Playa Blanca* and *Playa de Las Coloradas*. Built during the 18th century, it served as a lookout tower more than a real fortress. In fact, it dates back to an age in which the risk of pirate raids had diminished and large bastions were no longer necessary. Devastated by time and burnt by pirate raids carried out along the entire stretch of coast, this **castle** has been rebuilt and restored several times.

The circular outline of Las Coloradas Castle, dating from the 18th century, stands above the white houses dotted along the coast between Playa Blanca and Playa de las Coloradas.

The long, wide beaches on the south of the island are one of its loveliest features and are very popular with tourists who enjoy the sun and sea in these splendid bays framed by long sandy shores in a peaceful setting with a constant and pleasant light breeze.

PUERTO CALERO

Just to the south of *Puerto del Carmen*, Puerto Calero is a typical charming seaside village with lovely beaches. In 1989 a small but well-equipped tourist port was opened and has now become an important point of reference for sailing enthusiasts, as can be seen from the number of yachts, catamarans, boats and dinghies. Sea trips are most enjoyable from here and on the beautiful seabed diving enthusiasts will discover not only extremely varied and interesting marine flora and fauna, but also the quite impressive wreck of a sunken submarine.

A fairly new centre designed by Lluis Ibañez Margalef, Puerto Calero is a welcoming and verdant resort with many shops, top class hotels and, of course, boats of all kinds, including luxury ones, moored in the modern harbour.

CALETA
DEL MOJÓN BLANCO

Caleta del Mojón Blanco is a brilliant, bright little gem of a bay where the whitest sand is dotted with black rocks. Only a little more than 100 metres long, it represents one of the most delightful corners of Lanzarote, refreshed by constant soft breezes.

PUERTO DEL CARMEN

Puerto del Carmen, located slightly south of the centre of Lanzarote, only 10 kilometres from the airport, is undoubtedly the island's main tourist centre, as well as being the most popular and lively spot for nightlife. Originally a small and peaceful fishing village, during the 1970s it developed rapidly and intensively into a modern residential centre. In addition to the long sandy beaches (*Playa Blanca, Playa de los Porcillos, Playa de Matagorda*), a clear and usually quite calm sea and a pleasant climate, the town also has sporting and tourist facilities of the highest quality, and a wide range of many different types of restaurants, bars, discotheques and clubs mainly situated along the seafront. Every evening the *Avenida de las Playas* is enlivened by attractive lights, colour and music. Offshore, entertainment is provided once more by the magnificent, varied sights of the sea bed, an extremely rich and colourful world of marine creatures and flora.

Though still quite recently a simple and modest little fishing village, Puerto del Carmen has rapidly developed into one of the most popular tourist centres of Lanzarote, with a small harbour and crowded seafront, the Avenida de las Playas.

Before beginning our discovery of the products and typical dishes of Lanzarote it should be stated that, in general, there is no specific cuisine unique to the island, but rather there is a type of cookery common to all the Canary Islands while one or two have a more or less local speciality. Thanks to the wonderful climate and fertile soil – in ancient times the *Garden of the Hesperides* was thought to be located here – the Canaries are a verdant paradise. Thus in the orchards almond trees and citrus fruits flourish while golden leaves hang from the vines (Lanzarote and El Hierro, also famous for its figs, are outstanding in the sector of wines and viticulture). As well as favouring species native to temperate zones (the cycle of harvests can sometimes continue throughout the entire year) the soil and climatic conditions of the archipelago are suited to growing not only palm trees, sugar cane and even coffee plants, but also and especially to the cultivation of exotic fruits such as tender avocados, juicy pineapple, the delicate fruit of the guava, fresh mangoes and the scented papaya, while plantations of lichee, star fruit and other species are being developed.

But of all the varieties of fruit in the Canaries, the quantity and quality of the delicious sweet plantain are outstanding. Reflecting the generous natural climate enjoyed by the islands, this fruit is better than the usually larger but not so delicious banana, generally eaten in Europe and America. Excellent white, rosé and red table and dessert wines are produced in the archipelago, while the sweet and liquorish wines - so famous that even Shakespeare, Goldoni and Byron referred to them - are still in favour today. Production is not large but is increasing, and the quality is good. The wines are strong, produced from a single grape type, generally of native vines grown on sunny, volcanic slopes and often at surprising heights for the latitude and climate (even up to 1,700 metres!). Despite the sometimes serious lack of rain, cultivation of the vines in such extreme conditions is possible due to the ability of the volcanic soil, especially the layer of ash and lapillus known as picón, to absorb humidity from the air. At night the ground absorbs the humidity carried by the western trade winds – known as the "horizontal rain"

– and conserves it during the long sunny days. However, given such unusual conditions, it has obviously been necessary to develop fairly original methods of cultivation and ways of training the vines that are often labour intensive and vary from island to island. In compensation, the dry, fresh air especially on the higher levels, means that it is quite unnecessary to artificially treat the vines, to the benefit of the wines produced. On Lanzarote, the most easterly island, slightly more white wine is produced than red. The area of production covers almost the entire island itself including the areas of *Tinajo*, *Yaiza*, *San Bartolomé*, *Haría* and *Teguise*. The extremely dry but innately mild climate is negatively affected by the hot winds blowing from the nearby African continent and this gives rise to quite strenuous techniques of cultivation. Cone-shaped holes, large enough for the vine to establish its roots, have to be manually dug into the volcanic soil that covers the island at a depth ranging from only 2 cm to 2 metres. In addition, and still manually, dry-stone walls of volcanic rock are built in a semi-circle 7cm. high to protect the buds from the burning winds from the Sahara. The range of wines includes dry white (10.5°) with a perfume of exotic fruits, similar to sweet wines, a sweet amber *Moscatel* and a pale *Diego* (12.5-14°), a name local to *Vijariego*. As well as rosé wine, piquant and highly scented red wines are produced (11°). The dulce clásico is produced abundantly as the *Malvasia* grape flourishes here, as well as the liqueur (both 15°). The classic spumante (espumoso) is also good, made with less than 85 per cent Malvasia or Moscatel grapes integrated with authorised white grapes (15-22°). And finally a range of the best-known and tasty regional dishes of this quite spicy but unpretentious cuisine. First comes *gofio* – for centuries the islanders' bread, made from corn flour that is roasted and then, according to local preference, mixed with either water and sugar or goat's milk. Next is *sopa de cebolla*, an onion soup typical of Lanzarote, once an important producer of this vegetable, and *potage canario* – a vegetable soup with lentils of which various versions exist. For the meat course, roast or fried kid is delicious all year round cooked with herbs (cabrito in adobo or baifito) as well as tasty roast or fried Lanzarote

rabbit. The type of fish and shellfish available depends on the season but at almost any time of the year there are sardines (sardinas), also used in mixed salads, and fine fresh tuna (atun) still fished in the traditional manner with rods from the boat. Also native to these seas is the *vieja*, (parrot fish) a fish that is born male and dark grey in colour, turning into a female and bright red as it grows older. It is delicious grilled or, as it is often found in *Orzola*, dried in the sun and wind attached to a cord with normal pegs as if it were a handkerchief. Other fish that are easily found and caught along the coast are grouper (cherne), cobbler fish, barracuda, sole (lenguado), snapper, marlin, and many other species travelling in the wake of the current passing the Canaries. And to end, there are plenty of excellent sweets: *bienmesabe*, made from almonds, biscuits, eggs, sugar and Moscatel liqueur; *frangollo* is a mixture of water, flour, almonds, sugar and figs; lastly – puddings made from goats' milk. Typically, coffee in the Canaries is il *cortado*, made with less water and served with milk – but traditionally condensed milk is poured into the cup, instead of the usual hot milk, and no sugar is added.

LOCAL CRAFTS

The most traditional products of the Canaries reflect the history and customs of the islands as well as the lives of those who inhabited the archipelago long ago. Ceramics are the most frequent items, mainly for domestic use and often still decorated with reproductions of designs seen on ancient objects discovered locally. Sometimes made without the use of a wheel, the pieces are fired in ovens. Also splendid are the lacework, hand- and loom-woven embroidery and the characteristic small roses that are applied to tablecloths and rugs as well as some attractive carved wooden items. Today there are many markets and small shops exhibiting these craft products that, while delightfully naïve and charming, are also of great historic and cultural value in their simplicity.

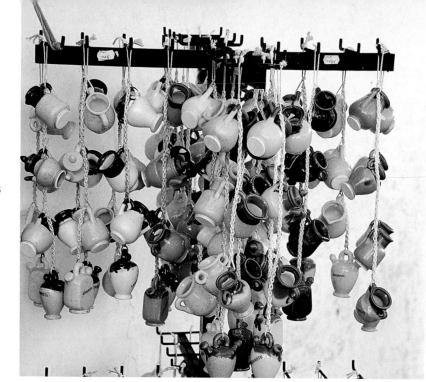